Handy Massachusetts Genealogy Handbook

Gary L. Morris

ISBN-13: 978-1505393682
ISBN-10: 150539368X

DEDICATION

For everyone who has a love and family and longs to establish a closer connection with them.

Notes

CONTENTS

Notes

Notes

Notes

About Genealogy Research in Massachusetts

Massachusetts has one of the oldest histories in the United States, and as such is rich in genealogical materials. Records have been generated since 1640, newspapers published from the mid-eighteenth century, and the oral histories of its native inhabitants passed on for thousands of years. As you can imagine there is a wealth of genealogical resources in Massachusetts. What we aim to do in this guide is to tell you:

What They are

Where to Find Them

How to Use Them

These valuable resources can be found both online and off, so we'll introduce you to some online databases and indexes, as well as the many brick-and-mortar repositories, societies and organizations that will help with your genealogical research in Massachusetts. In order to give you a more comprehensive understanding of these records, we'll also give you a brief history of "The Bay State", a state that has inspired its inhabitants to heroic acts of patriotism and national pride.

A Brief History of Massachusetts

Before the Europeans arrived, Massachusetts was populated by a number of small Native American tribes, numbering around thirty thousand. The first European settlement was established on the arrival of the *Mayflower*, which landed near Plymouth carrying 120 passengers and approximately 30 crew. Soon fishing and trading posts were established in the surrounding area, one of which would become the infamous Salem, the original capitol of Massachusetts.

The Native American tribes soon grew to resent the Puritan expansion, and rebelled beginning the Pequot War in 1637. Four New England colonies banded together to form the New England Confederation, which finally ended all Indian resistance.

Massachusetts Bay, Maine, and Plymouth were incorporated into a single colony in 1691. The colony had grown from its humble agricultural beginnings by the middle of the eighteenth century, and soon fishing and lumber production added to the national product.

War against the British exploded in April of 1775 when the Massachusetts militia (warned by Paul Revere during his famous ride) engaged the British army at Lexington and Concord. Patriots from other colonies flocked to Massachusetts to join the fight, and at the Battle of Bunker Hill on June 17, 1775, the soon to be first president of the United States George Washington took control of the patriot troops. The rest as you can say is history, and when a new constitution was drafted by a constitutional convention in 1780, a new era in Massachusetts and United States History had begun.

Rapid industrial expansion occurred after the Civil war in Massachusetts and throughout the United States. Many of the nation's new railroads were financed by Massachusetts capital, and though many residents left to head westwards, many more arrived from Europe.

Important Genealogical Dates in Massachusetts History

1620 - Colony established at Plymouth after Mayflower Voyage

1628 - Colony established at Salem

1632 - Boston becomes Capital of Massachusetts Bay Colony

1634 - Four Year War With Pequot Begins

1638 - Slave Ship *Desire* Arrives at Salem

1641 - Province of New Hampshire merged into Massachusetts Bay Colony

1680 - Province of New Hampshire Separated from Massachusetts Bay Colony

1692 - Salem Witch Hysteria Begins

1711 - Great Boston Fire, nearly 400 Buildings Destroyed

1721 - Small Pox Epidemic at Boston, 844 People Die

1741 - Final Separation of New Hampshire from Massachusetts

1754 - French and Indian War between France and England until 1760

1756 - North American War expands to Europe as Seven Years War

1775 – Revolutionary War gives birth to United States of America

1788 – Massachusetts Admitted to Union

1820 - Final Separation of Maine from the State of Massachusetts

Famous Battles in Massachusetts

The information contained in accounts and other documentation of famous battles can be very effective in uncovering the military records of your ancestor. They can tell you what regiments fought in which battles, and often include the names and ranks of many officers and enlisted men. Following are some of the most famous battles fought in Massachusetts and links to useful information about them.

Battles of Lexington and Concord, 1775

Battles of Lexington and Concord, 1775:
http://www.theamericanrevolution.org/battledetail.aspx?battle=1

Battle of Chelsea Creek, Suffolk County, 1775

Battle of Chelsea Creek, Suffolk County:
http://www.theamericanrevolution.org/battledetail.aspx?battle=114

Battle of Bunker Hill, Charlestown, Massachusetts, 1775

Battle of Bunker Hill, Charlestown, Massachusetts, 1775:
http://www.theamericanrevolution.org/battledetail.aspx?battle=5

Common Massachusetts Genealogical Issues and Resources to Overcome Them

Boundary Changes: A major issue in genealogical research in Massachusetts are historical boundary changes. It can be frustrating to be searching for an ancestor's record in one county when in fact it is housed in a neighboring one due to boundaries being changed over time. The **Atlas of Historical County Boundaries** can help you to overcome this issue. It provides a chronological listing of every boundary change that has occurred in the history of Massachusetts.

Atlas of Historical County Boundaries: http://publications.newberry.org/ahcbp/documents/MA_Consolidat ed_Chronology.htm#Consolidated_Chronology

Name Changes: Surname variations, changes, and misspellings can impede genealogical research. It is important to check every spelling variation possible. Soundex, a program that indexes names by sound, is a useful tool for that, but it can't be completely relied on as some name variations result in different Soundex codes. You will need to **get creative with surname variations** and spellings in order to cover every possibility. For help with surname variations read our instructional article on **How to Use Soundex**.

get creative with surname variations: http://obituarieshelp.org/blog/?p=634

How to Use Soundex: http://obituarieshelp.org/blog/?p=505

Massachusetts Genealogical Organizations and Archives

Genealogical resources include not only records, but the organizations that house them, or can direct you to them. These institutions include: *Archives, Libraries, Genealogical Societies, Family History Centers, Universities, Churches, and Museums.* Following are links to their websites, their physical addresses, and a summary of the records you can find there.

Archives

Massachusetts State Archives – vital records early period – present, passenger lists, military records, probates, adoptions, Native and African-American resources.

Secretary of the Commonwealth
Massachusetts Archives
220 Morrissey Blvd.
Boston, MA 02125

617-727-2816
Fax: 617-288-8429
Email: archives@sec.state.ma.us

Massachusetts State Archives:
http://www.sec.state.ma.us/arc/arcgen/genidx.htm

University of Massachusetts Amherst Libraries – vital records, church records, records of the *Mayflower*, land records, tax records, city directories, and marriage records.

154 Hicks Way, Amherst,
MA 01003, United States
+1 413-545-0284
Website:
http://guides.library.umass.edu/content.php?pid=9449&sid=81419

Massachusetts State Library – town reports, vital records series, historical newspapers, city and town directories, voters lists, tax valuations, family histories

State Library of Massachusetts
24 Beacon Street
State House, Room 341
Boston, MA 02133
617-727-2590

Special Collections
State House, Room 55
617-727-2595

Massachusetts State Library: http://www.mass.gov/anf/research-and-tech/research-state-and-local-history/genealogical-resources.html

Boston Public Library - a comprehensive collection of New England newspapers, governmental records, family and town histories, city and town directories, and more.

Boston Public Library
700 Boylston St.
Boston, MA 02116

Reference: 617-859-2270
Boston Public Library: http://www.bpl.org/

Massachusetts Genealogical and Historical Societies

Genealogical and historical societies have access to extensive catalogues of genealogical data. They are also able to offer expert guidance for genealogical researchers. Many members are professional genealogists who are most willing to share their expertise in finding ancestors.

New England Historic Genealogical Society – almost 3,000 searchable online databases with information on nearly 300 million individuals; includes vital records, social Security Death Index, immigration records, military records, wills, burial records, and court records.

99-101 Newbury St.
Boston,MA 02116, USA
Tel: 888-296-3447

New England Historic Genealogical Society:
http://www.americanancestors.org/home.html

Massachusetts Society of Mayflower Descendants – a variety of genealogical resources including probate indexes, incorporation documents, and Mayflower passenger lists.

175 Derby St. #13
Hingham, MA 02043-4036
781-875-3194
Email: info@massmayflower.org

Massachusetts Society of Mayflower Descendants:
http://www.massmayflower.org/

Daughters of the American Revolution – Revolutionary War pension lists, cemetery records, patriots database, county histories, surnames database.

1776 D Street NW
Washington, D.C. 20006
Tel: (202) 628-1776

Daughters of the American Revolution:
http://services.dar.org/public/dar_research/search/?tab_id=0

Massachusetts Historical Society – presidential papers, abolitionist manuscripts and photographs, American Revolution resources, maps, and diaries.

1154 Boylston Street,
Boston, MA 02215, United States
Phone:+1 617-536-1608

Massachusetts Historical Society: http://www.masshist.org/

Massachusetts Family History Centers

The Family History Centers run by the LDS Church offer free access to billions of genealogical records for free to the general public. They also provide classes on genealogy and one-on-one assistance to inexperienced family historians. Following is a link to a **Complete Listing of Massachusetts Family History Centers**.

Complete Listing of Massachusetts Family History Centers:
https://familysearch.org/locations/centerlocator

Additional Massachusetts Genealogical Resources

Massachusetts Mailing Lists

Mailing lists are internet based facilities that use email to distribute a single message to all who subscribe to it. When information on a particular surname, new records, or any other important genealogy information related to the mailing list topic becomes available, the subscribers are alerted to it. Joining a mailing list is an excellent way to stay up to date on Massachusetts genealogy research topics. Rootsweb have an extensive listing of **Massachusetts Mailing Lists** on a variety of topics.

Massachusetts Mailing Lists:
http://lists.rootsweb.ancestry.com/index/usa/MA/misc.html

Massachusetts Message Boards

A message board is another internet based facility where people can post questions about a specific genealogy topic and have it answered by other genealogists. If you have questions about a surname, record type, or research topic, you can post your question and other researchers and genealogists will help you with the answer. You must make sure to check back regularly, as the answers are not emailed to you. The message boards at the **Massachusetts Genealogy Forum** are completely free to use.

Massachusetts Genealogy Forum:
http://genforum.genealogy.com/ma/

Massachusetts Newspapers and Periodicals

The **Boston Public Library** has a massive database of historical and modern newspapers on microfilm, as does the **American Antiquarian Society** and the **State Library of Massachusetts**.

Boston Public Library: http://www.bpl.org/

American Antiquarian Society:
http://www.americanantiquarian.org/

State Library of Massachusetts:
http://www.mass.gov/anf/research-and-tech/oversight-agencies/lib/

Periodicals such as the *The Mayflower Quarterly* (1935-present) published by the **General Society of Mayflower Descendants** is a news magazine with articles on the Pilgrim experience and individual researched genealogies.

General Society of Mayflower Descendants:
http://www.mayflower.org/

Additionally there are those focusing on local histories such as *The Essex Genealogist* published by the **Essex Society of Genealogists** and the *Berkshire Genealogist* published by the **Berkshire Family History Association.**

Essex Society of Genealogists: http://www.esog.org/index.php

Berkshire Family History Association:
http://www.berkshire.net/~bfha/

Historical Massachusetts Maps and Gazetteers

Maps are necessary to genealogical research. They help us to locate landmarks, towns, cities, parishes, states, provinces, waterways and roads and streets. They also help us to determine when and where boundary changes might have taken place, and give us a visualization of the area we're researching in. For locating place names, a gazetteer is the best possible resource for any genealogist. Gazetteers are also sometimes called "place name dictionaries", and can help you to locate the area in which you need to conduct research. Below are links to the maps and gazetteers for research in Massachusetts.

Peabody GNIS Service – Massachusetts:
http://peabody.research.yale.edu/cgi-bin/Query.GNIS?ST=Massachusetts&SU=1

Color Landform Atlas – Massachusetts:
http://fermi.jhuapl.edu/states/ma_0.html

1985 U.S. Atlaso: http://www.livgenmi.com/1895/MA/

Massachusetts Hometown Locator:
http://massachusetts.hometownlocator.com/

Massachusetts Genealogical Records

<u>Birth, Death, Marriage and Divorce Records</u> – Birth, death, and marriage records are the most basic, yet most important records attached to your ancestor. They are generally referred to as vital records as they record vital life events. The reason for their importance is that they not only place your ancestor in a specific place at a definite time, but potentially connect the individual to other relatives. Below is a list of repositories where you can find Massachusetts vital records.

The Registry of Vital Records and Statistics – responsible for collecting, processing, correcting, and issuing copies of birth, death, marriage, and divorce records that occur in Massachusetts.

150 Mount Vernon Street #1,
Dorchester, MA 02125, United States
Tel: +1 617-740-2600

The Registry of Vital Records and Statistics:
http://www.mass.gov/eohhs/gov/departments/dph/programs/health-stats/vitals/obtaining-certified-copies-of-vital-records.html

Early Vital Records of Massachusetts – vital records from early era Massachusetts dating from 1600-1850.

Early Vital Records of Massachusetts: http://ma-vitalrecords.org/

Massachusetts State Archives – vital records dating from 1841-1910

Massachusetts State Archives:
http://www.sec.state.ma.us/arc/arcsrch/vitalrecordssearchcontents.html

Census Reports

Census records can lead you to other ancestors, particularly those who were living under the authority of the head of household.

U.S National Archives – Massachusetts census records from 1820-1880

Boston Federal Records Center
380 Trapelo Road,
Waltham, Massachusetts 02452-6399

Telephone: 781 663-0130
Fax: 781 663-0155
Email: waltham.reference@nara.gov

National Archives at Boston, MA
380 Trapelo Road
Waltham, Massachusetts 02452-6399
Toll Free: (866) 406-2379
Telephone: (781) 663-0144
Fax: (781) 663-0154
E-mail: boston.archives@nara.gov

U.S National Archives:
http://www.archives.gov/research/census/nonpopulation/massachu
setts.html

The **Massachusetts State Archives** holds state census schedules from 1855 and 1865 and federal census population schedules dated 1790 -1880, and 1900- 1920.

Massachusetts State Archives:
http://www.sec.state.ma.us/arc/arcgen/genidx.htm

Massachusetts Church Records

Church and synagogue records are a valuable resource, especially for baptisms, marriages, and burials that took place before 1900. The major religions in Massachusetts prior to 1900 were Congregationalists, Baptists, Methodists, Roman Catholic, and Episcopalians. Below are links to archives that maintain such records and modern day documentation and a few databases that can be viewed online.

Baptist – American Baptist Historical Society

2930 Flowers Road South,
Atlanta, GA 30341, United States
Tel: +1 678-547-6680
American Baptist Historical Society: http://abhsarchives.org/

Congregational – Congregational Christian Historical Society Library

14 Beacon St,
Boston, MA 02108
Tel: 617-523-0470
Congregational Christian Historical Society Library:
http://www.congregationallibrary.org/

Quakers – Rhode Island Historical Society

RIHS Library
121 Hope Street
Providence, RI 02906
401.273.8107
Rhode Island Historical Society: http://www.rihs.org/

Episcopal – Episcopal Diocese of Massachusetts

925 Commonwealth Avenue,

Brookline, MA 02446, United States
Phone:+1 617-482-4826

Episcopal Diocese of Massachusetts:
http://www.diomass.org/content/archives

Methodist – Boston University School of Theology Library

745 Commonwealth Avenue #2,
Boston, MA 02215, United States
Phone:+1 617-353-3034

Boston University School of Theology Libraryo:
http://www.bu.edu/sthlibrary/

Lutheran – Lutheran Archives Center, Philadelphia

7301 Germantown Ave.
Philadelphia, PA 19119-1974

Tel: 215.248.4616
Toll Free: 800.286.4616
Fax: 215.248.4577
Email: web@ltsp.edu

Lutheran Archives Center, Philadelphia:
http://ltsp.edu/lutheran-archives-philadelphia

Jewish – American Jewish Historical Society

15 West 16th Street,
New York, NY 10011, United States
Tel: +1 212-294-6160

American Jewish Historical Society: http://www.ajhs.org/

Presbyterian – Presbyterian Historical Society

425 Lombard St
Philadelphia, PA 19147
Tel: (215) 627-1852

Presbyterian Historical Society: http://www.history.pcusa.org/

Roman Catholic – Archdiocese of Boston

66 Brooks Drive,
Braintree, MA 02184, United States
Tel: +1 617-254-0100

Archdiocese of Boston:
http://www.bostoncatholic.org/Archives.aspx

Massachusetts Military Records

Massachusetts has a long history of armed conflict, and there is a wealth of military records available to genealogists. Below are a number of links to websites and archives that contain them.

Massachusetts State Archives – service records from the War of 1812, Shay's Rebellion, and the Spanish American War dating from 1643-1783.

Massachusetts State Archives:
http://www.sec.state.ma.us/arc/arccol/colidx.htm

Massachusetts Military Museum and Archives – National Guard records from 1636, Civil War volunteers records, soldiers and sailors records 1774-1940.

91 Everett St,
Concord, MA 01742
Phone: 978-369-4807
Email: ng.ma.maarng.mbx.museum@mail.mil

Massachusetts Military Museum and Archives:
http://states.ng.mil/sites/MA/resources/museum/default.aspx

Martha's Vineyard Soldiers and Sailors List – transcriptions of the Muster Rolls of individuals from Martha's Vineyard who served in the Revolutionary War

Martha's Vineyard Soldiers and Sailors List:
http://history.vineyard.net/dukes/msswr.htm

American Local History Network - 1840 Census of pensioner's revolutionary or military services

American Local History Network: http://www.alhn.org/

Bigelow Society – Listing of men and officers who served in King Philips War

Bigelow Society: http://bigelowsociety.com/rod/soldiers.htm

Civil War Soldiers and Sailors System – Civil War records of army and navy enlisted men and officers who served in both the Union and Confederate forces.

Civil War Soldiers and Sailors System: http://www.nps.gov/civilwar/soldiers-and-sailors-database.htm

Massachusetts Cemetery Records

As convenient as it is to search cemetery records online, keep in mind that there are a few disadvantages over visiting a cemetery in person. They are:

- Tombstone information may not always be accurately transcribed

- The arrangement of the graves in a cemetery can be crucial as family members are often buried next to each other or in the same grave. This arrangement is not always preserved in the alphabetical indexes that are found online.

With that information in mind, the following websites have databases that can be searched for Massachusetts Cemetery records.

Massachusetts Tombstone Transcription Project – tombstone transcriptions from the entire state with an index that is searchable by county

Massachusetts Tombstone Transcription Project link: http://www.usgwtombstones.org/massachusetts/massachu.html

Find a Grave – over 100 million grave records can be searched on this site. Search can be conducted by name, location, or cemetery name.

Find a Grave: http://www.findagrave.com/

Interment.net - A free online database containing cemetery records from thousands of cemeteries around the world. Consists of approximately 4 million cemetery records.

Interment.net: http://www.interment.net/

Billion Graves – as the name implies, you can search a billion records including headstone photos, transcriptions, cemetery records, and grave locations.

Billion Graves:
http://billiongraves.com/pages/search/index.php#cemetery

Massachusetts Obituaries

Obituaries can reveal a wealth about our ancestor and other relatives. Often things such as occupation, organization or club memberships, and former places of residence are included. You can search our **Massachusetts Newspaper Obituaries Listings** from hundreds of Massachusetts newspapers online for free.

Massachusetts Newspaper Obituaries Listings:
http://obituarieshelp.org/massachusetts_newspaper_obituaries.html

Massachusetts Wills and Probate Records

Massachusetts probate records govern the probate of wills, administration of estates, and the appointment of guardians. Since the 1630's they have been under the control of the county courts. From the 19th century onwards, name changes, divorces, adoptions, and domestic relations came under the jurisdiction of probate and family courts. The records are available at county level from county clerk's offices, while records from the 17th century can be found in the following:

- **Massachusetts Archives Collection**
  http://www.sec.state.ma.us/pre/preidx.htm

- **Suffolk County probate index** (for Essex County)
  http://catalog.hathitrust.org/Record/008729804

- **Suffolk Files**
  http://salem.lib.virginia.edu/archives/Suffolk.xml

- **Essex County Quarterly Court records**
  https://archive.org/details/recordsfilesofqu01mass

- **Middlesex Folio Collection**. http://massachusetts-genealogy.com/Middlesex-County-Historical-Records.cfm

Massachusetts Immigration and Naturalization Records

Naturalization records from Massachusetts county courts may still be at the county court, in a county or State archives, or at a regional archives serving several counties within a the State. If a Federal court oversaw the naturalization, declarations of intent, naturalization indexes, and petitions will usually be in the National Archives regional facility serving the State in which the Federal court is located. Some records for Massachusetts can be searched online at **Fold3**.

Fold3: http://www.fold3.com/documents.php?bc=22

Immigration records are plentiful and can be found at the following locations:

US National Archives –Passenger Lists of Vessels Arriving at Boston, MA, Jan. 1, 1902-June 30, 1906, Passenger Lists of Vessels Arriving at Boston, MA, July 1, 1906-December 31, 1920, Passenger Lists of Vessels Arriving at Boston, MA, 1891-1943, Crew Lists of Vessels Arriving at Boston, MA, 1917-1943.

US National Archives: http://www.archives.gov/research/immigration/immigration-records-1891-1957.html

Boston, Massachusetts Passenger Lists 1820-1954 – online records and indexes, and microfilmed records and indexes for Boston, Massachusetts passenger arrival records from 1820-1954

Boston, Massachusetts Passenger Lists 1820-1954: http://www.genesearch.com/boston/

Massachusetts State Archives – ships passenger Manifest 1848-1891

Massachusetts State Archives:
http://www.sec.state.ma.us/arc/arcsrch/PassengerManifestSearchContents.html

German Roots – New Bedford, Massachusetts Passenger Lists & Index 1902-1954 and Passenger Arrival Lists for Miscellaneous Atlantic, Gulf Coast & Great Lakes Ports 1820-1873. Listing contains names of passengers arriving in the Massachusetts ports of Barnstable, New Bedford, Dighton, and Hingham.

German Roots:
http://www.germanroots.com/miscports/newbedford.html

Massachusetts City Directories

City directories are similar to telephone directories in that they list the residents of a particular area. The difference though is what is important to genealogists, and that is they predate telephone directories. You can find an ancestor's information such as their street address, place of employment, occupation, or the name of their spouse.

A one-stop-shop for finding city directories in Massachusetts is the **Massachusetts Online Historical Directories page** which contains a listing of every available city and historical directory related to Massachusetts.

Massachusetts Online Historical Directorieso: https://sites.google.com/site/onlinedirectorysite/Home/usa/ma

Resources for Researching Female Massachusetts Ancestors

A woman's identity was often under that of her husband, and individual records for them can be difficult to locate. The following resources are effective in locating female ancestors in Massachusetts where traditional records may not reveal them.

Marriage and Divorce Records

The **Massachusetts State Archives** holds marriage records on microfilm from 1841-1901 (film 0961262 ff.) and from 1901-1905, (film 2057533 ff.)

Massachusetts State Archives: http://www.sec.state.ma.us/arc/

The **State Registrar of Vital Records and Statistics** holds microfilmed county records from Essex County Court – 1636-1795 (film 0877432 ff.) and Middlesex County Courts – 1600-1799 (film 1420474)

The following Divorce records are on microfilm at the State Archives.

- Massachusetts Council Divorce Records, 1760-1786 (film 0946895)
- Supreme Judicial Court index cards to divorce records, 1812-1867 (film 2027325 ff.)

The Superior Court in Northampton has the Hampshire County Superior Court index to divorces 1758-1960 on microfilm (film 2027325 ff.), while the General Court colony records, 1629-1777 are on microfilm (film 0954385 ff.) are at the Statehouse in Boston.

Website:
http://www.mass.gov/eohhs/gov/departments/dph/programs/health-

stats/vitals/

Bibliographies

- *Obligation and Opportunity: Single Maritime Women in Boston, 1870-1930*, Mary E. Beattie (University of Maine Press, 1994)
- *A Little Commonwealth; Family Life in Plymouth Colony*, John P. Demos (Oxford University Press, 1970)
- *The Women of the Mayflower and Women of Plymouth Colony*, Ethel Noyes, (Gryphon, 1971)
- *A Research Guide to the Massachusetts Courts and Their Records,* Catherine S. Menand (Massachusetts Supreme Judicial Court, Archives and Records, 1987)
- *Maiden Names from the Essex County, Massachusetts General Sessions*, Melinde Lutz Sanborn (New England Historical and Genealogical Register CXLIV, January 1990)

Selected Resources for Massachusetts Women's History

Fall River Historical Society
185 Salisbury St.
Worcester, MA 01609-1634

Plymouth Public Library
132 South St.
Plymouth, MA 02116

Library of the Boston Athenaeum
10 Beacon St.
Boston, MA 02108

Sophia Smith Collection
William Allan Nelson Library

Smith College
Northampton, MA 01063

Common Massachusetts Surnames

The following surnames are among the most common in
Massachusetts. The list is by no means exhaustive. If your surname
doesn't appear in the list it doesn't mean that you have no
Massachusetts connections, only that your surname may be less
common.

Abbott, Abell, Agar, Alcock, Aleworth, Andrew, Archer,
Aspinwall, Audley, Baker, Balston, Barsham, Bartlett, Bateman,
Baxter, Beamsley, Beecher, Belcher, Bendall, Benham, Biggs,
Black, Boggust, Boswell, Bosworth, Bourne, Bowman, Bradstreet,
Brand, Bratcher, Brenton, Bright, Browne, Buckland, Bugby,
Bulgar, Burnell/Bunnell, Burr, Burroughs, Cable, Cakebread,
Chadwick, Chambers, Chase, Chauner, Cheesebrough, Child,
Church, Clarke, Clough/Cluff, Coddington, Colbron, Colby, Cole,
Converse, Cooke, Cowlishaw, Crabb, Crafts, Cranwell, Cribb,
Crugott, Dady, Deekes/Dix, Devereux, Dillingham, Dixon,
Doggett, Downing, Dudley, Dutton, Edmunds, Eggleston, Ellis,
Elston, Eyens/Ijons/Irons, Fayerweather, Feake, Finch, Firman,
Fitzrandolph, Fox, Foxwell, Freeman, French, Frothingham, Gage,
Garrett, Gibson, Glover, Goldthwaite, Gosnall, Gosse/Goffe,
Goulworth, Gridley, Gyver, Haddon, Hale, Hall, Hammond,
Harding, Harris, Harwood, Hawke, Hawkins, Hawthorne,
Hesselden, Hoames, Hough/Hoffe, Hopwood, Horne, Hosier,
Howlett, Hudson, Hulbirt, Hutchins, Hutchinson,
James, Jarvis, Johnson, Jones, Kidby, Kingsbury, Knapp,
Knower, Lamb, Lawson, Learned, Leatherland, Legge, Lockwood,
Lynton, Lynn, Masters,Matson, Mayhew, Millett, Mills, Morey,
Morley, Morris, Morton, Moulton, Mousall, Munt, Nash,

Needham, Nowell, Paige, Painter, Palmer, Palsgrave, Parke,
Parker, Pattrick, Pelham, Pemberton, Penn, Penniman, Perry,
Phillips, Pickering, Pickworth, Pierce, Pond, Porter, Pratt,
Pynchon, Rainsford, Ratcliffe, Rawlins, Reade, Reading,
Reynolds, Richardson, Royse/Ryse, Ruggles, Sales, Saltonstall,
Sampson, Sanford, Saxton, Scott, Seaman, Seely, Sharpee,
Simpson, Smead, Smith, Smyth, Squire, Stearns, Stileman,
Stoughton, Sumner, Swaddon, Talmadge, Taylor, Tomlins, Turner,
Tyndal, Underhill, Vassall, Wade, Walker, Ward, Warren,
Waterbury, Waters, Webb, Weed, Weldon, Weston, Wilbore,
Wilkinson, Williams, Wilsby, Wilson, Wilton, Winthrop, Woods,
Woolrich, Wright.

ABOUT THE AUTHOR

Gary L. Morris worked from 2009 to 2014 as a professional researcher for a major player in the genealogy field. After tracing his family lineage back to 1683, he has decided to publish these helpful guides to share the valuable information he has discovered during his career to help others trace their family lineages. An avid genealogist himself, he hopes you will find this guide factual, thorough, helpful, and most of all, effective in helping you to find your family members.

www.ingramcontent.com/pod-product-compliance
Lightning Source LLC
Chambersburg PA
CBHW060442290526
45793CB00002B/545